Mr. C Takes a Vacation

Beverly Hoffman

Illustrated by Steve Pileggi

Dominie Press, Inc.

The development of the *Carousel Readers* was supported by the Reading Recovery project at California State University, San Bernardino. All authors' royalties from the sale of the *Carousel Readers* will be used to support various Reading Recovery projects.

Publisher: Raymond Yuen
Series Editor: Stanley L. Swartz
Editorial Assistant: Bob Rowland
Illustrator: Steve Pileggi
Designer: Pamela S. Pettigrew

Copyright © 1997 Dominie Press, Inc.

All rights reserved. No part of this publication may be reproduced or transmitted in any form or by any means without permission in writing from the publisher. Reproduction of any part of this book, through photocopy, recording, or any electronic or mechanical retrieval system, without the written permission of the publisher is an infringement of the copyright law.

Published by:

Dominie Press, Inc.
1949 Kellogg Avenue
Carlsbad, California 92008 USA

ISBN 1-56270-855-4
Printed in Singapore by PH Productions

2 3 4 5 6 7 IT 04 03 02 01 00

Mr. Cricket needed a change. He was bored, and he had nothing to do.

He was tired of playing in the woodpile.

He was tired of hopping in the garden.

The family that shared his home was going on a vacation. Mr. Cricket wanted to go on a vacation, too.

He packed his green backpack.
He packed a beach towel, his
sunglasses, and his swimsuit.

Mr. Cricket quickly and quietly hopped into the car, and off he went.

Several hours later the car stopped, the door opened, and out hopped Mr. Cricket. He looked around and saw the sand leading to a beautiful beach.

He headed toward the beach, wearing his swimsuit and sunglasses.

He lay on his towel
in the hot sun.

What a wonderful vacation he was having. The sun was setting, and the air was turning cool.

Mr. Cricket packed his backpack and went back to the car.

He fell asleep on the way home. He was a tired, but happy, cricket.

TITLES IN THE
Carousel Readers Series

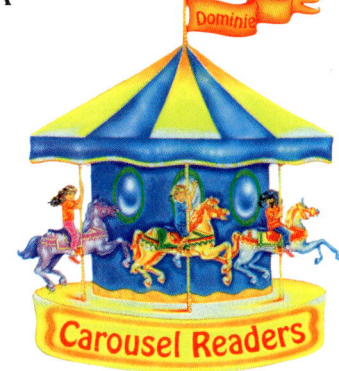

Carousel Readers Set A
Birthday Candles
Bubble Gum
Daniel's Basketball
  Team
The Desert
First Day of School
I Like to Play
My Dad Cooks
My Picture
In My Pocket
Flowers for Mom
Maybe I'll Be

Carousel Readers Set B
All Kinds of Food
Animals in the Desert
The Library
Lunch Time
Now I Ride
We Make Pizza
What Do You See?
What is Green?
Where is the School Bus?
Who Will Help?
The Zoo

Carousel Readers Set C
Butch, The Outdoor Cat
Can I Have a Lick?
Going Shopping
Going to the Beach
I Love Music
In My Garden
Look in Mom's Purse
My Dad Lost
  His Job
My Friend Alan
A Ride in the Country
Sharing Time

Carousel Readers Set D
Diana Made Dinner
Lost and Found
The Mail Came Today
My Skateboard
My Two Homes
Night in the Desert
Shapes
Something to Share
Water
What Fell Out?
What's On Your T-Shirt?

Carousel Readers Set E
A Bath for Patches
I'm a Good Reader
I Love Camping
Making Pancakes
Mick and Max
Moving to America
Mr. Cricket Finds a Friend
A Special Friend
Sunshine, The Black Cat
Two
Visiting Grandma
  & Grandpa

Carousel Readers Set F
The Clock that Couldn't
  Tell Time
Deep in the Woods
I Can Fly
I'm Sick Today
In My Bucket
The Messy Monsters
Mr. Cricket's New Home
People on the Beach
The Roller Coaster Ride
What Can We Do Today?
Where is Daniel?

Carousel Readers Set G
A Ball Game
I Can Do Many Things
Mumps
My Best Friend
Quack, Quack, Quack
Smokie
Spring
Swimming
Tea Party
Winter
Wishing for a Horse

Carousel Readers Set H
The Balloon
Dress Up
Feeding Time
The Great Car Race
I Like To Write
Kindergarten
Look at Me
Meet Mr. Cricket
Mr. Cricket Takes a
  Vacation
Stores
A Trip to the Zoo